Pentecost: Where the Spirit of God Is

Marlowe R. Scott

PENTECOST:
WHERE THE SPIRIT OF GOD IS

Marlowe R. Scott

Pearly Gates Publishing, LLC, Houston, Texas (USA)

Pentecost: Where the Spirit of God Is

Pentecost:
Where the Spirit of God Is

Copyright © 2020
Marlowe R. Scott

All Rights Reserved.
No portion of this publication may be reproduced, stored in an electronic system, or transmitted in any form or by any means (electronic, mechanical, photocopy, recording, or otherwise) without written permission from the author or publisher. Brief quotations may be used in literary reviews.

Print ISBN 13: 978-1-948853-08-8
Digital ISBN 13: 978-1-948853-09-5
Library of Congress Control Number: 2020918969

Scripture references are taken from the King James Version (KJV) of the Holy Bible and used with permission via Zondervan at Biblegateway.com. Public Domain.

For information and bulk ordering, contact:
Pearly Gates Publishing, LLC
Angela Edwards, CEO
P.O. Box 62287
Houston, TX 77205
BestSeller@PearlyGatesPublishing.com

Marlowe R. Scott

DEDICATION

It is an honor to dedicate
Pentecost: Where the Spirit of God Is
to my cousins:

Pastor Leroy Norman Harris

and

Elder Arlene Holden.

Pastor
Leroy Norman Harris

PASTOR LEROY NORMAN HARRIS – BIOGRAPHY

*"They are new every morning:
Great is thy faithfulness."*
~ Lamentations 3:23 ~

Pastor Leroy Norman Harris attended Victory Christian Fellowship Bible School in Wilmington, Delaware, under the leadership of Pastor Gary Whetstone. Pastor Harris is an Ordained Pastor by MSHCA and is the Founder and Pastor of Waves of Glory Christian Center.

Marlowe R. Scott

At a very young age, Pastor Harris became involved in ministry, as he regularly attended Sunday school and used his voice through song. The gift of music has enabled him to play as the Minister of Music in various churches in South Jersey, including Union Baptist Temple (Rev. Albert Morgan, Pastor), CCU Baptist Church (Bishop William Hargrove, Pastor), and St. Matthew Baptist. He not only ministered through music, he also assisted other ministries and established choirs. While working at Mission Teens in Norma, New Jersey, Pastor Harris was groomed as a Mission Outreach Minister.

When God called him to preach, Pastor Harris answered and established Waves of Glory Christian Center as a "church for all people." His message is simple:

"God is faithful."

That message encompasses all people in God's world, such as the brokenhearted, fatherless, and

Pentecost: Where the Spirit of God Is downtrodden. Through Waves of Glory Christian Center, God has been faithful to:

- Heal the sick.
- House the homeless.
- Mend broken hearts and families.
- Deliver drug addicts.
- Encourage the hopeless.
- Feed the hungry.
- Provide medicine, food, and clothing to those in need.
- Save the lost — locally and abroad.

Mission outreaches include:

- Santo Domingo
- Philippines
- Cuba
- Kenya
- Nigeria
- Mexico
- Haiti

Marlowe R. Scott

God blessed Waves of Glory Christian Center's outreach to build a well in Santo Domingo, where Pastor Harris continues to visit and spread the Word and sing songs of praise. In 2018, the Lord added a second church in Santo Domingo: "Olas De Glorias." Pastor Roberta Sosa was installed to lead that congregation in 2018.

Pastor Harris mentors and assists young men and women from time to time, showing them how to start their own business. He also owns and provides jobs in his transportation business in Sicklerville, New Jersey.

Pastor Harris is 62 years old at the time of this writing and has been blessed to be married to Missionary Barbara Harris for 36 years. They have four children, a son-in-law, and two grandchildren. He enjoys singing, spending time with his family, traveling abroad, and eating homemade food and desserts.

Pentecost: Where the Spirit of God Is

His favorite sayings are:

"God is faithful!"

and

"To God Be the Glory!"

~ Pastor Leroy Norman Harris, Pastor ~
Waves of Glory Christian Center
130 Oak Street
Williamstown, NJ 08094
Phone: (609) 647-1788

Marlowe R. Scott

Elder Arlene Holden

ELDER ARLENE HOLDEN – BIOGRAPHY

Elder Arlene Holden was born to the late James C. and Pearl F. Cooper in Stow Creek Township near Bridgeton, New Jersey. She is one of 13 siblings. At the age of three, she went to live with her maternal grandparents, Elder Charles E. and Ida J. Cooper, for 13 years.

Pentecost: Where the Spirit of God Is

She received her education in the Bridgeton and Millville, New Jersey areas. A genuinely caring, loving woman, she became a Licensed Practical Nurse in 1978. Elder Holden continued working in the medical field for 34 years.

In 1958, she married the late Elvin Powell, Jr. From this union, there are three children. She has one daughter-in-law, grand, great-grand, and great-great-grandchildren. Later in life, she married the late Elder Harmon Holden, adding four stepsons and their wives, grand, and great-grandchildren.

At the age of 23, she received Jesus Christ as her personal Savior and thanks God for victory through His Holy Word:

"If any of you lack wisdom, let him ask of God."
~ James 1:5a ~

She answered the call to ministry in 1982. On March 25, 1982, she—along with her cousin and brother in the Lord, Pastor Leroy Harris, now the Pastor of Waves of Glory Christian Center in Williamstown, New Jersey—delivered their first sermons.

Elder Holden was instrumental in the birth of St. John Pentecostal Church, which had its start in Springtown, New Jersey, after two weeks of revival. Her brother, the late Elder Hartley Pernell, Sr., was the first pastor. Later, the church relocated to its present location in Cedarville, New Jersey. Currently, Elder Holden holds the offices of Associate Minister, Church Clerk, and Sunday School and Bible Study Teacher at St. John Pentecostal Church.

When time permits, she enjoys sewing, crocheting, cooking, reading, and writing letters and poetry. She can quickly attest to the familiar lyrics of the song "If I Can Help Somebody":

Pentecost: Where the Spirit of God Is

*"If I can help somebody as I travel on,
then my living shall not be in vain."*

~~~~~~~~~~

Elder Arlene Holden wishes to express her appreciation to her cousin, Marlowe Scott, for allowing her to have a part in this great book. She prays God will continue to bless her in all of her endeavors.

Marlowe R. Scott

The following inspirational poem is a prime example of the creative gift Elder Holden has in expressing and witnessing through her words.

FOR ALL HE HAS DONE
Arlene Holden, 6/26/2020

For all He has done,
Take the time to remember
God gave His only Son.

God knew man would not be able
To save himself from sin.
Without God's redeeming plan,
We would never win.

The day of crucifixion
Should be clearly in our mind.
Oh, how the Savior suffered
To redeem all of mankind.

He was so badly beaten
In such a dreadful way.
His skin laid wide open,
As they kept striking Him that day.

Pentecost: Where the Spirit of God Is

They mocked and spat upon Him;
He never looked away.
He stood and said not a word
To save Himself that day.

They pressed a crown of thorns
Deep into His head,
And made Him carry the heavy cross —
Even though He bled.

They stripped Him of His robe of white
And gave Him a robe of red.
The accusation, "Jesus of Nazareth — King of the Jews"
Was placed above His head.

There He hung upon the cross
With nails through His hands and feet.
Even though death was near,
He showed His love and promised salvation to a thief.

They took a sword and pierced His side
To make sure He had died.
Blood and water came gushing out;
He was the King of the Jews — that was no doubt.

Marlowe R. Scott

A day of mixed emotions.
A day full of gloom.
They took His body from the cross
And laid Jesus in a tomb.

To the sepulcher, the women came
To anoint their Blessed Lord.
The stone the soldiers had secured
Was rolled from the door.

Just like Jesus said,
On the third day He rose.
And there lay in the tomb,
Nothing but His grave clothes.

"He is not here!"
They were frightened by the words they heard.
He is risen from the dead,
Like the Bible said.

He is alive!
Oh yes, Jesus lives!
To all who believe,
Salvation He will give.

Pentecost: Where the Spirit of God Is

Oh, won't you let Him
Come into your heart?
He wants all of you,
Not just a part.

JESUS SAVES!

Marlowe R. Scott

ACKNOWLEDGMENTS

First and foremost, I am thanking and praising our Lord and Savior Jesus Christ for saving me! As a member of His family, I know I must strive to be more like Him and use the talents I have been blessed with to witness, share, and love others. Knowing Jesus and sharing the Good News have been such rich experiences as my spiritual growth continues to prosper.

Secondly, to the gift of my children and my youngest, Angela R. Edwards: As the Lord uses her talents of writing, publishing, and witnessing through her two publishing houses—Pearly Gates Publishing, LLC and Redemption's Story Publishing, LLC—she has enriched the lives of men, women, and children as they read and apply the messages in over 100 published books!

Thirdly, to my two cousins—Pastor Leroy N. Harris and Elder Arlene Holden—who the Lord led me to dedicate the words of *Pentecost: Where the Spirit of God Is*. They both continue to preach God's Word, love and encourage others as they build up men, women, and children for membership in the body of Jesus Christ. The lives they have ministered to are countless!

To God Be the Glory!

Marlowe R. Scott

PREFACE

The inspiration for this book came on Tuesday, May 26, 2020, after hearing a sermon preached by Pastor Leroy Harris the previous Sunday. He is Pastor of Waves of Glory Christian Center in Williamstown, New Jersey.

His sermon was about Pentecost and when the Holy Spirit came to the earth after Jesus ascended into Heaven. During this inspired sermon, Pastor Harris mentioned the Azusa Street Mission Revival in Los Angeles, California during the early 1900s. That instantly piqued my spiritual interest. I learned the mission church established on Azusa Street is recognized as the renewed birth of the Global Pentecostal Movement, which began in America. Many well-known churches, ministries, outreaches, and, most importantly Christian converts have resulted worldwide.

Pentecost: Where the Spirit of God Is

Again, I mention the word "revival" in the Azusa Street Mission Revival name. That word immediately quickened my spirit! I recall the revivals churches held while I was growing up. There would be aunts, uncles, cousins, and some preachers from local churches and their members.

These were the old-fashioned tent revivals held in hot, humid New Jersey summer months. There were wooden folding chairs, cardboard fans or just newspapers to keep cool and swat flies and mosquitoes. Often, there were few musical instruments, except the occasional guitar to accompany familiar hymns.

They were much different than the revivals of today, which are often held in large churches or stadium. Now, there are pianos, organs, drums, guitars, elaborate sound systems, videos, and livestreaming on cell phones, computers, and other devices.

Marlowe R. Scott

Although change has occurred, the Word of God and the purpose of the Holy Spirit remain the same. The theme texts found in both the Old and New Testaments prove that to be TRUE!

Pentecost: Where the Spirit of God Is

THEME TEXTS

"And it shall come to pass afterward, that I will pour out my Spirit upon all flesh; and your sons and your daughters shall prophesy, your old men shall dream dreams, your young men shall see visions."
~ Joel 2:28 ~

"If you love Me, keep My commandments. And I will pray to the Father, and He shall give you another Comforter, that He may abide with you forever."
~ John 14:15-16 ~

"But ye shall receive power after that the Holy Ghost is come upon you: and ye shall be witnesses unto Me both in Jerusalem, and in all Judea, and in Samaria, and unto the uttermost part of the earth."
~ Acts 1:8 ~

Marlowe R. Scott

INTRODUCTION

This book, *Pentecost: Where the Spirit of God Is*, is being written during truly turbulent times in America:

- ❖ Civil unrest.
- ❖ Racism.
- ❖ Inadequate governmental leadership.
- ❖ A pandemic virus that has caused over 200,000 deaths.
- ❖ Houses of Worship closed because of health dangers.
- ❖ Schools—from nurseries to universities—are closed.
- ❖ Businesses—both small and large—have downsize or worse…closed.

With all of that and more, there is a CRITICAL need for a spiritual revival and a Pentecostal experience once again that continues globally…and LASTS!

Pentecost: Where the Spirit of God Is

After hearing a sermon by Pastor Leroy N. Harris on Sunday, May 24, 2020, my interest was heightened to the point of researching "Azusa Street Mission Revival" on the internet. There was loads of information available. Being an avid reader and author, I then went online and purchased a book on the topic. Although there were many from which to choose. I was led to one written by Cecil M. Robeck, Jr. The title is appropriately, *The Azusa St. Mission & Revival: The Birth of the Global Pentecostal Movement* (Thomas Nelson, Publisher).

That historical treasure contains extensive information about the Azusa Street Mission & Revival, only some of which is included in this book. The workings of the Holy Spirit in converts is varied and will be shared later.

The message of the Holy Spirit being manifested then and still NOW, proves that the indwelling and baptism of the Holy Spirit is able to impact a needful world.

As Jesus Christ promised, the Holy Spirit (also known as the Holy Ghost) did come in Acts 4:31.

"And when they had prayed, the place was shaken when they were assembled together, and they were all filled with the Holy Ghost, and they spake the Word of God with boldness."

Scripture was fulfilled and the resulting spread of the Gospel with new converts and witnesses began!

The Holy Bible has many qualities Christians receive as they grow spiritually. TimA familiar text that many Christians study is found in Galatians 5:22-23, where the Fruit of the Spirit is listed as:

Pentecost: Where the Spirit of God Is

- ❖ Love
- ❖ Joy
- ❖ Peace
- ❖ Patience
- ❖ Kindness
- ❖ Goodness
- ❖ Faithfulness
- ❖ Gentleness
- ❖ Self-Control

Each of those qualities were clearly demonstrated by Jesus while He ministered on earth and are to be a part of every Christian's life. It must be noted that some of the fruit may be harder to incorporate into one's life; however, it is wise to pray for each quality because it is The FRUIT of The SPIRIT. It is one fruit with many seeds, like an apple or orange.

Marlowe R. Scott

TABLE OF CONTENTS

DEDICATION VI
PASTOR LEROY NORMAN HARRIS – BIOGRAPHY VII
ELDER ARLENE HOLDEN – BIOGRAPHY XII
FOR ALL HE HAS DONE XVI
ACKNOWLEDGMENTS XX
PREFACE XXII
THEME TEXTS XXV
INTRODUCTION XXVI
THE BEGINNING 1
THE HOLY SPIRIT'S INSPIRATIONAL MESSAGES TO ME 4
PEN YOUR INSPIRATION 9
THE PROMISES OF THE SCRIPTURE 11
DENOMINATIONS STEMMING FROM AZUSA 16
T.D. JAKES KEEPING WITH THE GREAT COMMISSION 18
MISSION DESCRIPTION 20
THE END OF AZUSA STREET REVIVAL MISSION ... 23
PENTECOST – A POEM 27
CONCLUSION 29
CLOSING PRAYER 31
GLOSSARY 32
ABOUT THE AUTHOR 34

Pentecost: Where the Spirit of God Is

THE BEGINNING

The world has too many religions, denominations, and spiritual beliefs to be counted. There are Baptist, Methodist, Catholic, Judaism, Presbyterian, and countless others. Some are heavy-laden with rules and customs dating back centuries ago.

THIS book, however, is about the Christian experience of the coming of the Holy Spirit manifesting itself in America without regard to denominations.

When I initially thought of Pentecost, the memories of Pentecostal and Holiness churches I was familiar with while growing up in South Jersey came to mind. I was raised Methodist, and there were a few Pentecostal and Holiness churches in the surrounding towns. The women dressed differently for church than we did. Most of the women wore long, black skirts and dresses in dark colors. Most often, they did not wear jewelry and makeup. The men and pastors did, however, dress like my pastor.

One of the most significant differences was that their worship services were much louder. Their singing, speaking in tongues, shouting, shaking tambourines, and clapping could be heard before one would even enter through the church doors. Also, their worship services were much longer, and they often regularly attended more than one service every Sunday. Another characteristic I did not fully understand was that often, members would shout so much, they fell to the floor and rolled side to side. Some called them "Holy Rollers," which I did not fully comprehend until I was older.

This is an opportune time and distinct honor to share with you some valuable family Pentecostal history!

Pentecost: Where the Spirit of God Is

As stated in her biography, my cousin Arlene Holden was raised by her grandparents, Elder Charles E. and Ida J. Cooper, for part of her life. Her grandfather, Elder Cooper, was instrumental in founding the first Black Pentecostal church in Bridgeton, New Jersey, which is Bethel Pentecostal Church. Elder Cooper had heard Bishop Ida B. Robinson, Founder of Mt. Sinai Holy Church of America, Inc., preach under the anointing of the Holy Ghost. After hearing Bishop Robinson, he knew that was what he, as well as others, needed.

Elder Cooper asked Bishop Robinson to bring such a church with its fiery message to Bridgeton, New Jersey. The Bishop agreed, and Elder Cooper was one of three people to make up Bridgeton's first Pentecostal church. They named it Bethel Pentecostal, which was first located on Warren Street then moved to Grove Street. After many years under Elder Henry Satchell, the church membership moved to 128 South Avenue, Bridgeton, where it still stands today.

Marlowe R. Scott

THE HOLY SPIRIT'S INSPIRATIONAL MESSAGES TO ME

As we continue to share workings of the Holy Spirit, I can attest to times when I have been touched and influenced by this extraordinary Spiritual Gift!

One of the most amazing experiences I had with the Holy Spirit was after I prayed and was seeking to compose a poem to support my daughter, Angela Edwards, and her *God Says I Am Battle-Scar Free* series of books.

I was alone in a room at a Poconos resort in Pennsylvania looking out the glass doors that faced a mountain. I had paper and pen nearby when suddenly, I picked up the pen and my hand quickly started writing. Immediately, I composed the poem, "Abuse Is Not Love!" I recall excitedly calling Angela and sharing the experience and poem. It has been

Pentecost: Where the Spirit of God Is printed in the books of the series and is a constant source of inspiration in the *Battle-Scar Free* books!

Another instance was when I desired to do something special for my husband. His favorite song is "His Eye Is on the Sparrow," and I wanted to write a book dedicated to him.

One day, a small paperback book, which was on a small cabinet in the hallway of my home, was turned upside down and had been there for a long time. I picked it up and found the story of Ethel Waters — the actress and well-known singer who sang "His Eye Is on the Sparrow" as she traveled with spiritual crusades! Her story and blessings were perfect for another Spirit-inspired book, *I AM Cares: His Eyes Are on the Sparrow.*

Needless to say, my husband was beyond words when I presented him a copy!

This next blessing stems from being raised in a loving Christian home. I have been in church since infancy and know numerous hymns and spirituals. One is based on the plentiful harvest and few laborers, which is also referenced in the New Testament Book of Luke 10:2a. *"Therefore, said He unto them, 'The harvest truly is great, but the labourers are few': pray ye therefore the Lord of the harvest, that He would send forth labourers into His harvest."*

As a woman raised in New Jersey's farming country, I understand labourers and harvest times very well. The song kept replaying in my mind, and an inspirational urge came to write once again. The title of that published book is *Plentiful Harvest: Fertile Ground*.

Most recently, while the country and the world are experiencing severe problems with hatred, illnesses, deaths, and mistreatments of individuals — especially Black Americans — the inspiration came

Pentecost: Where the Spirit of God Is

to have others share their experiences through poetry. From that came another literary resource for those voices to be "heard."

In collaboration with my daughter, Angela, we offered the opportunity for others to have their poetic interpretations included in the book. The invitation was extended to adults as well as children. The result is poems by authors from seven years old through me, at 76 years of age!

God, through His Holy Spirit working, helped with the publication of *Poetic Voices: Seeking Solidarity During Racial Transitions*. The book is a wealth of true instances of abuses and unfair treatment of all kinds, expressed in words. I constantly thank and praise God for the gifts and talents He has given me as I use them to inspire and nourish others!

Marlowe R. Scott

Abundant blessings came as each of the above-mentioned books (plus others) received Best-Seller recognition when introduced on Amazon.

Pentecost: Where the Spirit of God Is

PEN YOUR INSPIRATION

In this space, write about times when the Holy Spirit spoke to you and the action you took.

Marlowe R. Scott

THE PROMISES OF THE SCRIPTURE

God, in the Ten Commandments given to Moses, has two essential commands which deal with LOVE! Paraphrased, they are: to LOVE God with all our hearts and soul, and to LOVE our neighbor as we LOVE ourselves. They are mentioned because the Holy Spirit came to ALL mankind.

Again, the Holy Spirit came to ALL—not just Jews. Jesus ministered to and healed people wherever He went. There were the sick, poor, sinners, and more who were touched by Him. This included men, women, and children. Likewise, the same is true of Pentecost coming on American soil. Those who were among the early members of Azusa Street Mission who experienced the Pentecost blessings were multi-racial and multi-cultural. Later, as the experience grew, there would be divisions which will be shared later.

The Holy Spirit was first promised by the Old Testament prophets and appeared after Jesus Christ had risen, walked the earth again, and met with His disciples in Jerusalem. The disciples were told to tarry in Jerusalem. After Jesus' ascension to Heaven, the promised Spirit came like tongues of fire and touched those disciples with that Holy Ghost fire.

The first Pentecost experience describes the people who had been touched by those fiery tongues as sounding like they were drunk. They were loud and strange languages were heard.

Some of the qualities the Holy Spirit gives are:

- ❖ Comforter
- ❖ Intercessor

Pentecost: Where the Spirit of God Is

- ❖ Advocate
- ❖ Counselor
- ❖ Helper
- ❖ Enabler of:
    - Understanding
    - Faithfulness
    - Righteousness
    - Truth
- ❖ Distinguishing of Spirits
- ❖ Speaking in Tongues

Fast-forward to the early 1900s.

William J. Seymour, the son of a slave, left the south and headed north. He met and stayed with a family near Los Angeles, California. Seymour began holding small devotional times with that family. Word of what was happening there eventually spread because of his profound messages and teachings. He was truly gifted.

In time, it became necessary to find a larger place to study and share because people were gathering outside to hear. A rustic building with dirt floors on Azusa Street was found. The building had straw-strewn floors, planks on nail kegs for seats, and a shipping crate served as the first pulpit. That humble beginning became known as the Azusa Street Mission Revival, Los Angeles, California. There, visions of the Holy Spirit were visibly seen and felt by those who became converts to Christianity.

The book by Cecil M. Robeck, Jr. has many examples of what services were like at Azusa Street Mission. Services were loud and some called the people "Holy Rollers" because of their display of rolling on the floor when they were having highly spiritual experiences. The worship services often lasted late into the night, causing the neighbors to complain about being sleep-deprived. On one occasion, people threw rotten eggs at worshippers who routinely gathered outside the mission!

Pentecost: Where the Spirit of God Is

Nevertheless, as intended from the beginning, a renewed Pentecostal experience had reached mankind, as preachers and missionaries began spreading the good news of Salvation through Jesus Christ!

Marlowe R. Scott

DENOMINATIONS STEMMING FROM AZUSA

Missions, churches, and denominations from that humble Azusa Mission beginning are spread around the globe. Preachers and missionaries were sent to witness in foreign lands, near and far, including:

- ❖ Mexico
- ❖ Canada
- ❖ Western Europe
- ❖ Middle East
- ❖ Asia
- ❖ West Africa
- ❖ Northern Russia

In America, churches and missions stemming from Azusa Mission were also started in:

Pentecost: Where the Spirit of God Is

- San Jose, San Francisco, and San Diego, California
- Salem and Portland, Oregon
- Denver and Colorado Springs, Colorado
- Chattanooga, Tennessee
- Norfolk, Virginia.

Marlowe R. Scott

T.D. JAKES KEEPING WITH THE GREAT COMMISSION
(Matthew 28:18-20)

While doing research on Azusa Mission, I discovered that the well-known American pastor, Rev. T.D. Jakes' name came up. His vast ministry definitely includes the message to love one another and serve the masses, without regard to creed, color, age, and more. Following is a prestigious recognition Rev. Jakes received.

~~~~~~~~~~

The Azusafest 2016 winner of The William Seymour Award was Rev. T.D. Jakes. The event is a three-day Gospel Music celebration commemorating the Azusa Street Revival in Los Angeles, California. The award is given to senior leaders in ministry exhibiting characteristics of the Lord's humble servant, Rev. William J. Seymour.

Pentecost: Where the Spirit of God Is

The Potter's House is in Dallas, Texas, where Rev. T.D. Jakes is pastor, was recognized for the church bringing leaders together for racial reconciliation—the all-inclusive basis for equal respect and love for all of our fellowman.

Racial reconciliation is a paramount need today (as shared earlier). Christianity is offered to all of the racial groups God made, which stemmed from the first man, Adam, and his mate, Eve.

Marlowe R. Scott

MISSION DESCRIPTION

Bible scholars, preachers, and those who attend church and bible studies will attest to God often using the lowly and poor to bless mankind. Wealth is not a prerequisite. Examples are the birth of Jesus Christ born in a stable and David, a shepherd boy, who killed the giant Goliath and later became a king.

The Azusa Street Mission fits into the rugged, poor category. It was a boxy, two-story building that had been on fire but not completely destroyed. The first pews were redwood planks supported by nail kegs. There was an assortment of chairs, benches, and backless stools. The first pulpit was a wooden packing crate covered with a cotton cloth.

When they had meetings, songs I am familiar with were sung, such as:

Pentecost: Where the Spirit of God Is

- ❖ How I Love Jesus
- ❖ The Name of Jesus is So Sweet
- ❖ Jesus Savior, Pilot Me

In today's Christian music, you can hear the songs of the Gaithers Singers or Sandy Patti based on those beliefs associated with the original messages and outreach of Azusa Street Mission.

It is recorded that a woman named Jennie Moore was able to play the piano at the Mission after an inspiration to sit down and play the keys—without ever having lessons!

Sadly, just as Jesus' ministry on earth did not last for many years, it was the same for the initial tremendous growth of the Azusa Street Mission pastored by Rev. William J. Seymour. Before telling that part of the decline, brief examples of present-day pastors follows.

~~~~~~~~~

There are ministries today founded on many principles and beliefs of the Azusa Street Mission. Reverends Pat Robertson, Oral Roberts, Kenneth and Gloria Copeland, and the renowned T.D. Jakes (mentioned earlier) credit the Azusa Street Mission for their beginnings. A sampling of the few other denominations said to have similar origins are:

- ❖ Assemblies of God
- ❖ Pentecostal Assemblies of the World
- ❖ United Pentecostal Churches
- ❖ Victory Outreach

Pentecost: Where the Spirit of God Is

THE END OF AZUSA STREET REVIVAL MISSION

Like some churches today, as other people from "traditional religions" joined the Azusa Street Revival Mission, they wanted some of the practices incorporated into the Mission that were from their former churches.

Some issues and discrepancies that presented themselves were:

- ❖ Water baptism or sprinkling of water.
- ❖ The definition of sanctification and divorce.
- ❖ Women preachers leading churches.
- ❖ As some of the other churches had officers and more organization than Azusa, others desired tithing, incorporation, and other practices.

From its beginning, the Azusa Mission depended on God to supply its needs and, of course, they were supplied. Tithing was not an issue. Azusa received donations and the original members worked and shared their talents as in Bible times.

Eventually, men as well as women, left the Azusa congregation and started churches in other cities, states, and overseas.

All of those reasons and personal conflicts caused a decline in membership at Azusa Street Mission. Rev. Seymour died September 28, 1922. Then, his wife, Jennie Seymour, led the declining mission until her death.

The original building was demolished years ago. The site is now marked with an historical marker, which simply declares:

Pentecost: Where the Spirit of God Is

"AZUSA ST. MISSION
Site of the Azusa St. Revival from 1906 to 1931
Cradle of the Worldwide Pentecostal Movement"

In closing, I remain confident that the Holy Spirit directed me to choose Pastor Leroy N. Harris, who has visited the Azusa Street Mission site, as one to whom this book is dedicated. In his biography, Pastor Harris states that his church, Waves of Glory Christian Center, was established to be a "church for all people."

Elder Arlene Holden, another faithful servant of God, has her own messages and witnessing evidenced by those who know her. She quickly remembered Azusa's spiritual importance to the Pentecostal Movement in America and the world, as I spoke with her about my inspiration for this book.

Marlowe R. Scott

PRAISE GOD FOR THE HOLY SPIRIT!
PENTECOST IS STILL MOVING!

Pentecost: Where the Spirit of God Is

PENTECOST – A POEM
Marlowe R. Scott, June 2020

The God who created our Heaven and earth
Had a long-range plan from the beginning.
You ask how do I know?
Because the Holy Bible proves it is so!

It was prophesized in the Old Testament by Joel and others
That the Holy Spirit would come to man.
The promised fulfillment of the Holy Spirit was sent on Pentecost;
Tongues of fire came to believers while they were in Jerusalem.
The fiery tongues caused those who were touched to speak differently,
Which amazed all who heard them, but not clearly.
There was overwhelming shouting and praising,
So much that people said those praising were drunk.
However, the work of the Holy Spirit had begun,
As new Christian converts became followers of Jesus, God's Risen Son.

Centuries later in America, there also occurred a Pentecostal experience.
It came through the Azusa Street Mission in Los Angeles, California,
Through the preaching and teaching of Rev. William Joseph Seymour,
Which caused the far-reaching birth of a global Pentecostal Movement!

Rev. Seymour was used by the Holy Spirit to preach and further spread the Gospel story.
His messages caused those fiery tongues appear
To Christians and new converts saved, as praises and speaking in tongues were heard
By people who came from far and near to hear.

As God chose Rev. Seymour at the Azusa Street Mission to receive and spread His Word,
I am reminded that God often uses simple things to confound the wise.

The commission to go into all the world, preach the Gospel, and save the lost
Is a never-ending blessing, starting that first Day of Pentecost!

CONCLUSION

The Word of God in the Holy Bible never changes. From the Old Testament scriptures to the New Testament, the Holy Spirit enables mankind to accomplish the expansive mission of making disciples in all nations.

"Go make disciples of all nations, baptizing them in the name of the Father, Son, and Holy Spirit, teaching them to observe all things that I have commanded you and lo, I am with you always, even to the end of the age."
~ Matthew 28:19-20 ~

In these times, that command has not changed and is more critical than ever! The Pentecostal experience of receiving the baptism of the Holy Spirit cannot be matched by any earthly feeling.

There is still much work to do and responsibilities for each Christian. Because God is no respecter of person (as mankind is), everyone can contribute to the building up of the Kingdom of God while we have breath.

CLOSING PRAYER

Dear Heavenly Father,

This world You created is greatly blessed by You, Jesus Christ, and the Holy Spirit. You have always known how this sinful world would become. You knew we needed Your love and mercy to guide us every moment of every day.

We cannot thank and praise You enough!

As we individually and collectively do the work of spreading the Gospel, we seek to use those gifts You have given to us to go into all the world and tell others the Good News of Salvation and encourage them to come and join Your family.

Amen.

GLOSSARY

Baptism: Religious rite of sprinkling water onto a person's forehead or of immersion in water symbolizing purification or regeneration and admission to the Christian church.

Ethnic: Relating to a population subgroup (within a larger or dominant national or cultural group) with common national or cultural traditions.

Holy Roller: A member of a Christian group which expresses religious fervor by frenzied excitement or trances.

Holy Spirit: The third person of the Trinity; God as spiritually-active in the world.

Multi-ethnic: Relating to or constituting several ethnic groups.

Multi-racial: Made up relating to people of several or many races consisting of, representing, or combining members of more than one racial group.

Outreach: Activity of providing service to any population that might not otherwise have access to those services.

Pentecost: Where the Spirit of God Is

Pentecost: A Christian festival celebrating the descent of the Holy Spirit on disciples of Jesus after His ascension; held on the 7th Sunday after Easter.

Pentecostal: Relating to or denoting any of a number of Christian movements and individuals; emphasis on baptism in the Holy Spirit, evidenced by speaking in tongues, prophesying, healings, and exorcism; a member of a Pentecostal Movement.

Sanctification: Set apart as or declare as holy.

Speaking in Tongues: Speech addressed to God, but also as something that can potentially be interpreted into human language, thereby edifying the hearers.

Tambourine: A percussion instrument resembling a shallow drum with small metal disks in slots around the edge; played by being shaken or hit by the hand.

Tarry: To linger in expectation; wait; to abide or stay in or at a place.

Tithing: 10% of income given specifically to your local church.

ABOUT THE AUTHOR

Marlowe R. Scott was born 1944 to the late Carl and Helena Harris. She is the youngest of three and the sole surviving sibling, a mother of three, a grandmother of five, and a great-grandmother of twelve. As a child, Marlowe always loved animals and nature in general. Before attending school, she learned how to read and memorized many of the rhyming stories in Mother Goose books.

Pentecost: Where the Spirit of God Is

With her parents and brothers, Marlowe attended John Wesley Methodist Church in Bridgeton, New Jersey, where she learned hymns, went to Sunday School and Methodist Youth Fellowship, and sang in the Junior Choir. A special memory she has is when, during the Civil Rights Movement of the 1960s, she participated in a nonviolent march from the church to the Bridgeton County Courthouse steps.

Marlowe was taught the value of confidence early in her youth. The familiar words still ring true and are often spoken today by others:

*"You are no better than anyone else,
and nobody is better than you."*

Teachers enjoyed having her in classes, as she was intelligent, participated, and articulated very well. In 1962, when she was a Senior in Bridgeton High School, she was chosen to be the Lead Speaker in the graduation voice choir, which quoted a portion of Ecclesiastes 3.

Later, as a member of Friendship A.M.E. Church in Browns Mills, New Jersey, Marlowe taught Sunday School, sang in various choirs, ushered, and worked with the Missionaries. She was also the Pastor's Steward to the first woman pastor of the church. Because of her experiences, she was elected Lay President of the Atlantic City District of New Jersey of the 1st Episcopal District of the A.M.E. Church. The Atlantic City District had 31 churches she visited, and she was charged with coordinating events, as well as other religious activities.

Marlowe retired from the workforce after 33 years of government civil service. She has found her voice now through writing inspirational books and poetry. She has penned the following Best-Selling books, which are available through Pearly Gates Publishing's website and Amazon:

Pentecost: Where the Spirit of God Is

- ❖ Spiritual Growth: From Milk to Strong Meat
- ❖ Keeping It Real: The Straight and Narrow
- ❖ Believing Without Seeing: The Power of Faith
- ❖ Worth the Journey: The Train Ride to Glory *(A trilogy of the three listed above)*
- ❖ Never Alone: Intimate Times with Jesus
- ❖ Plentiful Harvest: Fertile Ground
- ❖ I AM Cares: His Eyes Are on the Sparrow
- ❖ Abiding is Not Hiding: Safe in His Arms
- ❖ Pentecost: Where the Spirit of God Is
- ❖ Talli's Ancestry Surprise: Beginning the Ancestral Search *(A children's/family book)*

A personal theme Marlowe has adopted for her life is the Serenity Prayer:

"God, grant me the **SERENITY**

to accept the things I cannot change,

the **COURAGE** to change

the things I can,

and the **WISDOM**

to know the difference."

Marlowe R. Scott